HENRY H. HOUSTON PUBLIC SCHOOL

ALLEN AND RURAL LANES

PHILADELPHIA, PA. 19119

LIBRARY

MEASUREMENTS
AND HOW WE USE THEM
by Tillie S. Pine and Joseph Levine
pictures by Harriet Sherman

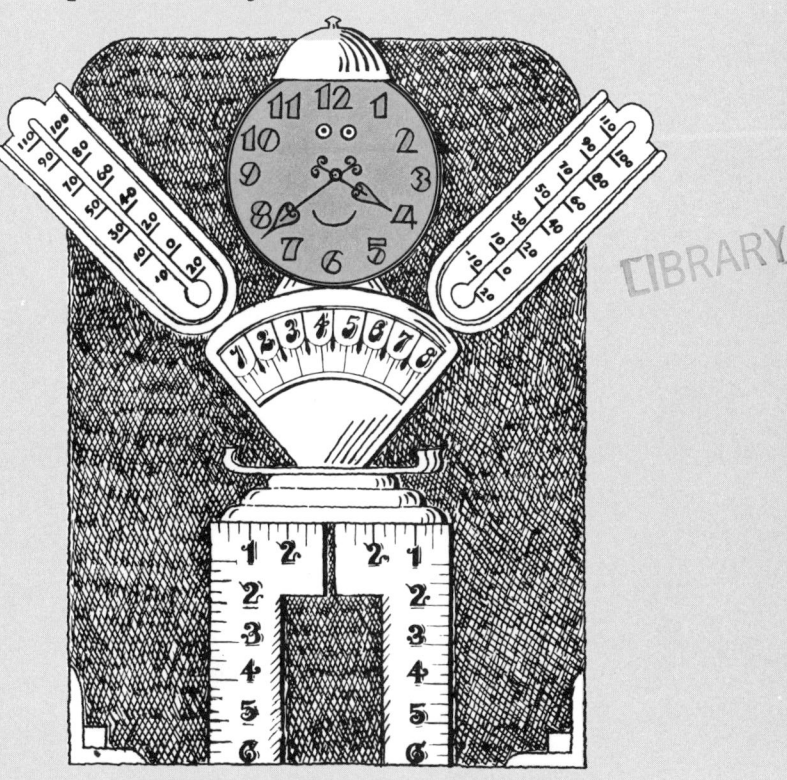

McGraw-Hill Book Company
NEW YORK ST. LOUIS SAN FRANCISCO DUSSELDORF
JOHANNESBURG KUALA LUMPUR LONDON MEXICO
MONTREAL NEW DELHI PANAMA RIO DE JANEIRO
SINGAPORE SYDNEY TORONTO

also by Tillie S. Pine and Joseph Levine

THE AFRICANS KNEW
THE CHINESE KNEW
THE EGYPTIANS KNEW
THE ESKIMOS KNEW
THE INDIANS KNEW
THE PILGRIMS KNEW
THE INCAS KNEW
THE MAYANS KNEW
AIR ALL AROUND
ELECTRICITY AND HOW WE USE IT
FRICTION ALL AROUND
LIGHT ALL AROUND
GRAVITY ALL AROUND
HEAT ALL AROUND
MAGNETS AND HOW TO USE THEM
SIMPLE MACHINES AND HOW WE USE THEM
TREES AND HOW WE USE THEM
SOUNDS ALL AROUND
WATER ALL AROUND
WEATHER ALL AROUND

MEASURING ALL AROUND
Copyright © 1974 by Tillie S. Pine and Joseph Levine.
Illustrations copyright © 1974 by Harriet Sherman.
All Rights Reserved. Printed in the United States of America.
No part of this publication may be reproduced,
stored in a retrieval system, or transmitted,
in any form or by any means, electronic, mechanical,
photocopying, recording, or otherwise,
without the prior written permission of the publisher.

Library of Congress Cataloging in Publication Data
Pine, Tillie S.
  Measurements and how we use them.
    SUMMARY: Projects and examples introduce various
  measuring devices and how to use them.
    1. Measuration—Juvenile literature.
  [1. Measuring] I. Levine, Joseph, date joint
  author. II. Sherman, Harriet, illus. III. Title.
  T50.P53   389'.1   73-6626
  ISBN 0-07-050084-3

For Mary,
whose enthusiasm and dedication as teacher
cannot be measured

MEASUREMENTS AND HOW WE USE THEM

When you want to know—
　　how soon your birthday will be,
　　how high you can reach,
　　how tall you are,
　　how much your dog weighs,
　　who is heavier, you or your best friend,
　　how warm your bathtub water is—

you really want to find out about—
　　the passing of time,
　　how far or near, how tall or short,
　　how heavy or light, how hot or cold
　　things are.

Of course, you can guess, and the answers might be—soon, fast, slow, heavy, high, low, short, hot, cold, very far or very near.

But—when you use these words, you will not get careful answers. You need something to help you *measure* these things to get careful *measurement*s.

As you read this book you will find out—
　　how we measure things,
　　what we use to help us do this and—
　　why we need to measure things carefully.

In each picture, someone is measuring something.
Why?
What is being used to help get
a careful measurement?

HOW LONG A TIME?
HOW SHORT A TIME?

Mother sometimes says that you may play outdoors for one hour. Can you guess how long it takes for this time to pass?

First, see if you can guess how long it takes for two minutes to pass. Ask your friend to look at a clock while you do this. Close your eyes and say "Go!" When you think two minutes have passed, open your eyes and say "Stop."

Ask your friend how much time has passed on the clock. Did you guess correctly? You probably did not.

Now ask your friend to close *his* eyes
and to guess the passing of two minutes
while *you* look at the clock.
Did he guess correctly?

So—when you go out to play,
do you think it is easy to guess
the passing of one hour?
You need a clock or a watch
to help you measure
the passing of time
carefully.

Look at your clock again.
The shorter hand, which is the *hour*-hand,
moves around the clockface very slowly.
The longer hand, which is the *minute*-hand,
moves around the clockface faster.

When the minute-hand makes one complete
turn around, 60 minutes pass. And—during that
time—the hour-hand moves from
one hour-numeral to the next hour-numeral.

Some clocks and most watches have still another
hand called the *second*-hand, which
moves around much faster than the other two.
When the second-hand makes one complete
turn around, 60 seconds pass.
And—during that time—the minute-hand moves
from one minute-mark to the next minute-mark.

We call the *hour* (hr.), the *minute* (min.)
and the *second* (sec.) our units of measure
in the passing of time. And—anyone who
uses them can get a careful measurement.

Do you know how many hours pass from
the time you get up in the morning until you
go to bed at night? How many hours pass
while you are sleeping?
Use your clock to help you
measure the passing of these times.

Do you know how many minutes and seconds
pass when you walk from
your home to school?
Use your watch
to help you
measure this.

How else do we measure the passing of time?

When you say to your friend, "I'll see you in two days," you are using the "day" as a measurement.

When you say to your friend, "I am eight years old," you are using the "year" as a measurement.

We call the *day* and the *year* other units of measure in the passing of time. And—anyone who uses them can get a careful measurement.

So you see—we measure the passing of time in different ways and—we use different units of measure to help us.

Who uses these units to help them measure the passing of time carefully?

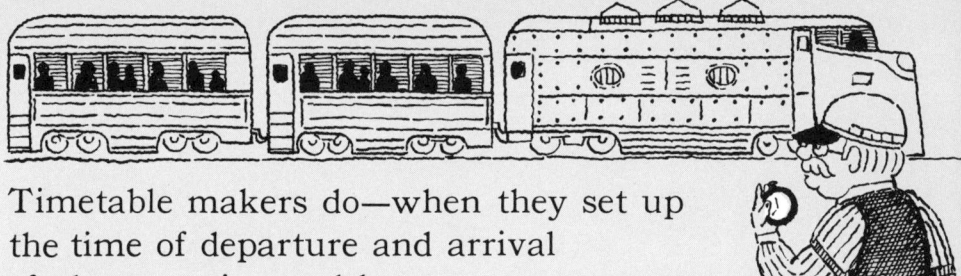

Timetable makers do—when they set up the time of departure and arrival of planes, trains and buses.

Space scientists do—when they program space flights.

Government officials do—when they plan their work and keep records.

Manufacturers do—when they decide how much time they need to—
cook foods for canning
heat materials to make glassware
and dishes, plastics, steel and glass.

Timekeepers do—when they keep the time of football, baseball and basketball games.

Racing officials do—when they use special watches, called stopwatches, to time races.

And you do—when you want to know—
how long it takes you to complete a puzzle
how long it takes you to make chocolate pudding
how many hours you are in school each day
how many years have to pass before you can vote on Election Day.

HOW FAR? HOW NEAR?

You have walked from your house to the curb many, many times. But—do you know just how long this distance is?

Start at your house and take *short* walking steps straight out to the curb. Count the number of steps you take. You might say that the distance from your house to the curb is the number of steps you walk.

Now walk the same distance again, but—this time take *longer* steps. What do you find?

You take fewer steps than before! Your count is different each time.

Do you think stepping is a good way to measure distance? Is there a better way?

You can use something to help you measure distance more carefully. Get a 12-inch ruler. We call it a *one-foot* ruler. It is marked off in lines and numerals. We call the distance between one numeral and the next numeral—*one inch*.

Place your ruler on the sidewalk. Have the one-inch end touch the wall of your house. Make a chalk mark on the ground at the 12-inch end. You have measured *one foot* of the distance between your house and the curb.

Now move your ruler straight out and have the one-inch end touch the chalk mark. Make another mark on the ground at the other end of the ruler.

You now have measured *two feet* of the distance. Keep measuring and counting this way until you measure the entire distance from the wall of your house to the curb. Are there any inches left over after the last chalk mark you can make?

How many feet did you count?

How many inches?

The number of feet and inches that you get is the distance between your house and the curb.

Now—ask your friend to use the ruler in the same way.
But—have him measure the distance *from the curb to the wall* of your house.

Your friend gets the same number of feet and inches that you did. So you see—a ruler is a measuring instrument that you can use to measure distance carefully.

We call the *foot* (ft.) and the *inch* (in.) our units of measure of distance. And—anyone who uses them can get a careful measurement.

Who uses these units to measure distance carefully?

Carpenters do—when they measure the wood they cut to get correct sizes for making furniture and for building houses.

Sports officials do—when they measure the lengths of shotputs and the heights of jumps. They use a special kind of long ruler called a *tape measure* to find the winners.

Tailors do—when they measure people to get the right sizes of clothing. They use a tape measure to do this. Sometimes tailors use a ruler that is 36 inches long. We call this a *yardstick*. A yard (yd.) is another unit of measure of distance.

Carpet layers do—when they measure the size of rooms for carpeting.

You do—when you and your friends want to find out how far each of you can throw a ball and—when you want to know who grows the most in height each month, you or your friends.

Have you ever wondered how long the block is on which you live?

Of course, you can use your ruler to measure it. But—would you be surprised to know that you can use your bicycle to help you do this?

Put a chalk mark on your bicycle tire where it touches the ground. Make a mark on the ground at this spot. Roll your bicycle forward slowly until the mark on the tire meets the ground again. This is one complete turn of the wheel. Put a mark on the ground at this spot.

Use your ruler to measure the distance between the two marks on the ground. This shows you how far your bicycle goes when the wheel makes one complete turn.

If your bicycle goes 7 feet, how far will it go when the wheel makes two turns? It will go 14 feet. In three turns it will go 21 feet.

Now—start from one end of your block and roll your bicycle slowly to the other end. Watch the chalk mark on your tire. Count the number of turns your wheel makes.

Now you can easily find out how many feet long your block is.

You know that one turn of the wheel measures 7 feet. If your wheel makes 30 turns, how many feet long is your block?

How wide is your street? Most streets are 50 feet wide.

When you ride your bicycle 20 blocks and you ride across 19 streets, we say you ride about one mile.

One mile is 5,280 feet long.

We call the *mile* (mi.) another unit of measure of distance. And—anyone who uses it can get a careful measurement.

How do drivers of cars,
trucks and buses find out how
many miles they travel when they drive?

They read the dial of the *odometer* (o-dom'-eter)
on the dashboard. Next time you
ride in a car, ask the driver to show it to you.

Remember when you measured the length of your
block with your bicycle? You counted the
number of turns your wheel made.
The odometer, too, uses the turns of the car
wheels to "measure" the distance the car travels.
The odometer has an attachment to the front
wheel. This attachment "counts" the turns
of the wheel and—the numerals on the odometer
show the number of miles the car travels.

When you ride in a car, write down the numerals you read on the odometer—when the trip starts and when it ends. Do not include the last numeral on the right. This tells only the tenths of a mile. You can subtract the smaller number from the larger one to get the distance you traveled on the trip.

We use a special instrument that uses radio waves to help us find out how far away storms, clouds and ships at sea are. This instrument also shows how high and how far away airplanes are flying.

We call this instrument—*radar*.

So you see—we measure distance, far and near, in different ways and— we use different kinds of instruments to help us do this.

You might want to keep a record of how much your weight changes each month.

To do this, you use another kind of measuring instrument—your bathroom scale.
Weigh yourself. Write your weight on your record. Repeat this each month and you will see how much your weight changes as you grow up.

Would you like to know how your scale works? Do this and you will understand. Hang a strong rubberband on the knob of your kitchen cabinet. Tie a cord around a small book. Hook a paper clip to the cord. Hook the other end of the clip to the rubberband. Let the book hang freely. What happens?

The weight of the book stretches the rubberband. Measure the length of the stretched rubberband with your ruler. How long is it?

Take off the small book and hook a larger book to the rubberband. Let this book hang freely. Now measure the length of the stretched rubberband again.

You see that the weight of the larger book stretches the rubberband more than the smaller book did. The larger book is heavier than the smaller one and it stretches the rubberband more.

When you step on your bathroom scale, you make something stretch inside the scale. It is not a rubberband that stretches. It is a thick spring.

This spring is attached to a bar. The bar also has a thin stretched spring attached to it. The other end of this spring is attached to the cogwheel which is attached to the dial. The picture shows you this.

When you step onto the scale, the thick spring stretches. This releases the stretched thin spring. The cogwheel and the dial turn. When the dial stops moving, the pointer shows your weight in numerals. It tells you the number of *pounds* you weigh.

We call this scale—a *spring scale*.

Now use your spring scale to find out how much your dog weighs. Hold your dog in your arms and step on the scale again.

How much do both of you weigh together? Subtract your weight from this weight. How much does your dog weigh?

Now—
use your bathroom scale and find
the weight of different things in your house—
Mother's iron
your skates
your book bag with your school books in it.

You can use your scale to get a careful measurement of the weight of many different things.

You can also have fun playing a weight-guessing game with your friends. Guess how much each friend weighs. Have each one step on your scale to find out his weight.

How close were you at guessing correctly?

Who else uses spring scales to measure weights carefully?

Some storekeepers do—when they weigh fruits and vegetables for their customers.

Postal clerks do—when they weigh letters to find out how many stamps are needed for mailing.

Some laundry workers do—when they weigh bundles of laundry to make sure they do not overload the washing machines.

We use another kind of scale to measure weights carefully.

The next time you visit a large food market, look at the scale the clerk uses.

This is a special kind of weighing scale.
It is a scale *without* a spring.
We call it—a s*pring*le*ss* s*cale.*
This scale has a bar in it with a pointer attached to the bar. When the clerk weighs fruits or vegetables on this scale,
the bar inside the scale tilts.
The more the weight, the more the bar tilts.
The less the weight, the less the bar tilts.
And—the pointer moves to the numeral
on the dial to show the weight in *pound*s.

To show a more careful weight, there are lines between the numerals on the dial.
These lines show ounces, which are parts of a pound. There are sixteen ounces in each pound.

We call the *pound* (lb.) and the *ounce* (oz.) our units of measure of weight.
And—anyone who uses them can get a careful measurement.

Who uses springless scales?

Butchers do—when they weigh meats.
Some storekeepers do—when they weigh vegetables, fruits, fish and sliced meats. They want to know the weights of these foods to help them find how much to charge their customers.

State troopers do—when they use a huge scale to measure the weight of loaded trucks to make sure that they are not overloaded. Some filled trucks weigh as much as 18,000 pounds.

For this kind of heavy weight, we use another unit of measure—a *ton*.
And—
2,000 pounds make one ton.

So—an 18,000 pound truck weighs nine tons.

Zookeepers do—when they, too, use a huge scale to measure the weight of elephants and other large animals. This helps the keepers take care of the animals' health.

Would you be surprised to know that if there are 27 boys and girls in your class and they could be weighed together on one big scale, they would weigh about one ton?

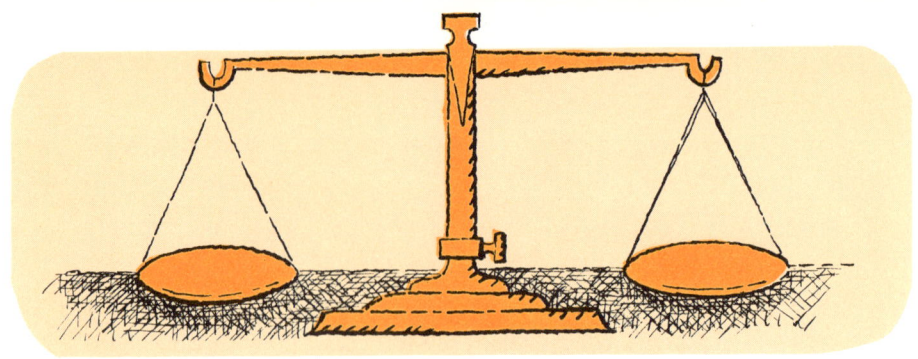

We make still another kind of weighing scale to measure the weight of things.

Visit your neighborhood drugstore.
Ask the druggist to show you the weighing scale that he uses when he fills some prescriptions.

You can do some simple things to help you understand how *this* scale works. Hold a penny in one hand and a dime in the other.

Does the penny feel as heavy as the dime?
It is not easy to tell this way.

So—do this. Lay a flat-sided pencil on the table. Place a 12-inch ruler across the pencil with the 6-inch mark right over it.

Is the ruler straight across without touching the table? If not, move it a little until it is.

We say the ruler is now balanced.

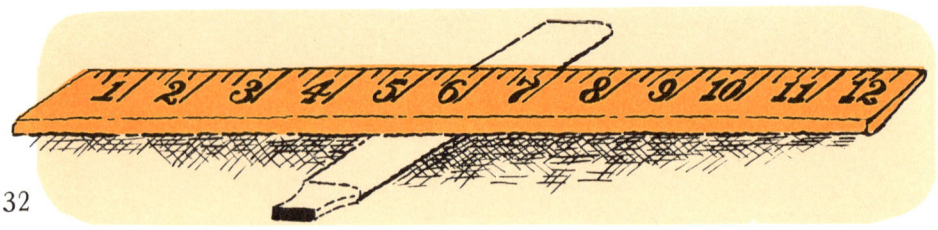

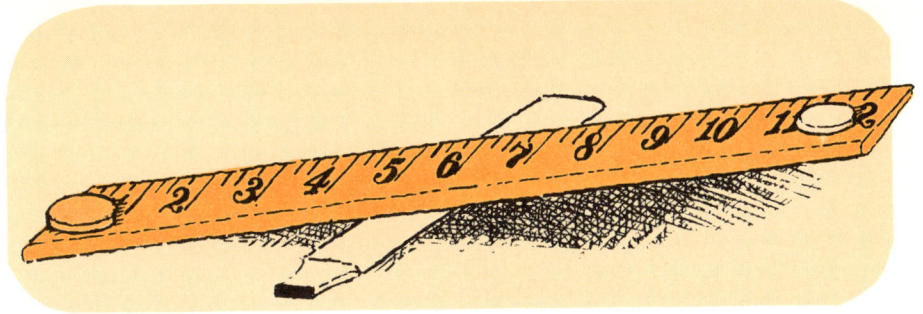

Put the dime at the edge of one end
of your ruler. The ruler dips down at this end.
Now put the penny at the other end.
This end dips down and the other end goes up.

What does this show you? It shows you that the
penny is heavier than the dime.

You can find out how many paper clips,
together, will have the same weight as one penny.

Clear your ruler and balance it on the pencil
again. Put your penny on one end of the ruler.
Pile as many clips as you need, one on top of
the other, on the other end until the ruler balances.

How many clips did you use?
You probably used five clips.
You can say that five paper clips
have as much weight as one penny or—
five paper clips "weigh" one penny.

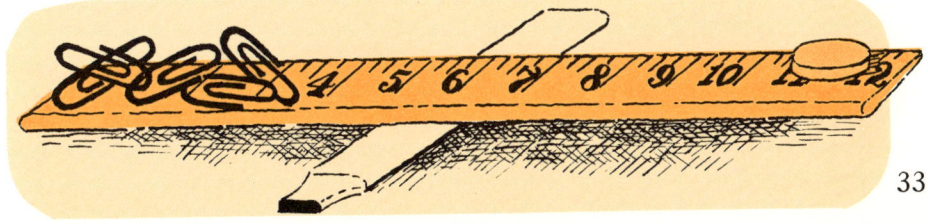

You could call your penny your "unit" of measure of weight.

Use your "unit of measure" in weighing other small things—tacks, small nails, rubberbands, toothpicks.
So you see—you used your ruler and pencil as a "balancer" to help you weigh things.

You could even call this balancer
—a *balance scale*.
Do you think that you can use *your* balance-scale and *your* unit of measure to weigh larger things and heavier things carefully?

To weigh heavier things, we have factory-made balance scales and we use them in the same way that you used *your* balance scale.

We put a weight on one platform of the factory-made scale. We put the thing we weigh on the other platform. When the scale balances, we know that we have a careful measurement.

So—when the druggist wants to weigh two ounces
of a certain chemical, he puts a
2-ounce weight on one platform of his
balance-scale. He puts the chemical on the other
platform until the scale balances.
Now he knows that he has weighed out two
ounces of the chemical carefully.

Who else uses balance-scales?

Clerks in some food stores do—when a customer wants two pounds of nuts, the storekeeper places a 2-pound weight on one side of the balance-scale. He puts the nuts on the other side until the scale balances.

Jewelers do—when they use a small balance-scale and small weights to weigh the gold, the silver and the diamonds they need to make jewelry.

Doctors do—when they use a lever-balance scale to find out how much you weigh when you visit their offices. This scale has a bar with a sliding weight on it. When the bar is balanced, the numerals on the bar show your weight in pounds and ounces.

Now you know how many different things are weighed. You also know how we use different types of scales to help us do this carefully.

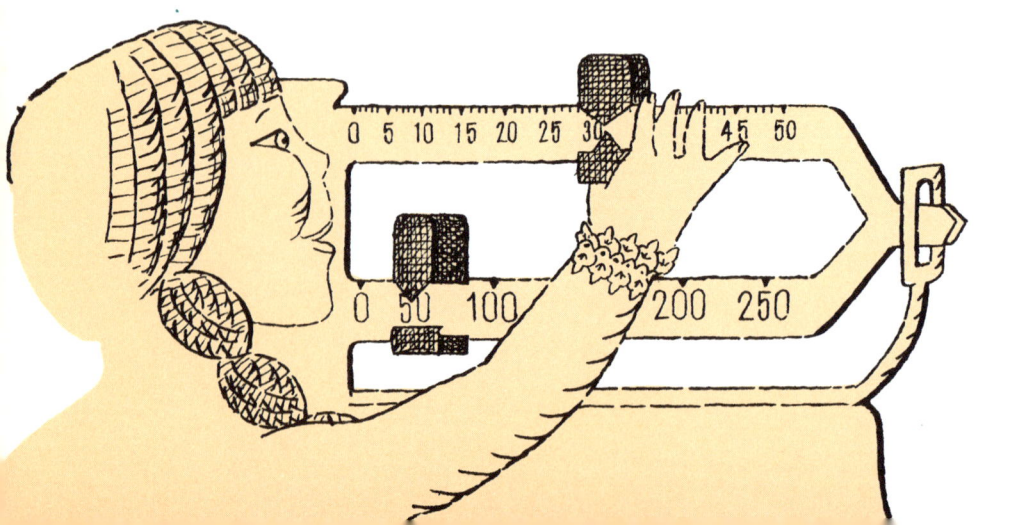

HOW HOT?
HOW COLD?

Sometimes when you go outdoors, in the wintertime, you say that the air *feels* very cold.

When you go outdoors on a hot day, in the summertime, you say that the air *feels* very warm.

Do your feelings really measure just *how* cold or *how* warm the air is? Is there a better way?

Of course, you can listen to the weatherman on TV and he will tell you how cold or how warm the air is outdoors.

When he tells you this, we say he is giving you the temperature.

How does *he* find the temperature?
He uses an outdoor thermometer to help him.

How does a thermometer work?

Get an outdoor thermometer and look at it.
You see a closed glass tube with a bulb
at the bottom. You also see a red liquid
in the bulb and in part of the tube.
This liquid is colored alcohol.

The tube is attached to a narrow flat holder.
There is a line of numerals on the holder next
to the tube. Now—fill one bowl with warm
water—but not hot—and another with cold water.
Place the bulb part of the thermometer
in the warm water.

Do you see the alcohol *rising* in the tube?
What makes this happen?

The warm water does. It makes the alcohol in
the thermometer warmer. The alcohol expands.
This pushes it higher in the tube.

When the alcohol stops rising, write down the
numeral that is next to the top of the red line.
Now—place the bulb part of the thermometer
in the cold water.

Do you see the alcohol going down in the tube?
What makes *this* happen?

The cold water cools the alcohol and it contracts.
The alcohol in the tube goes back toward the
bulb. When it stops moving, write down
the numeral that is now next to the top of
the red line.
These numerals tell you how warm the warm
water is and how cold the cold water is.

When you use a thermometer to measure water
this way, you are taking the temperature
of the water.

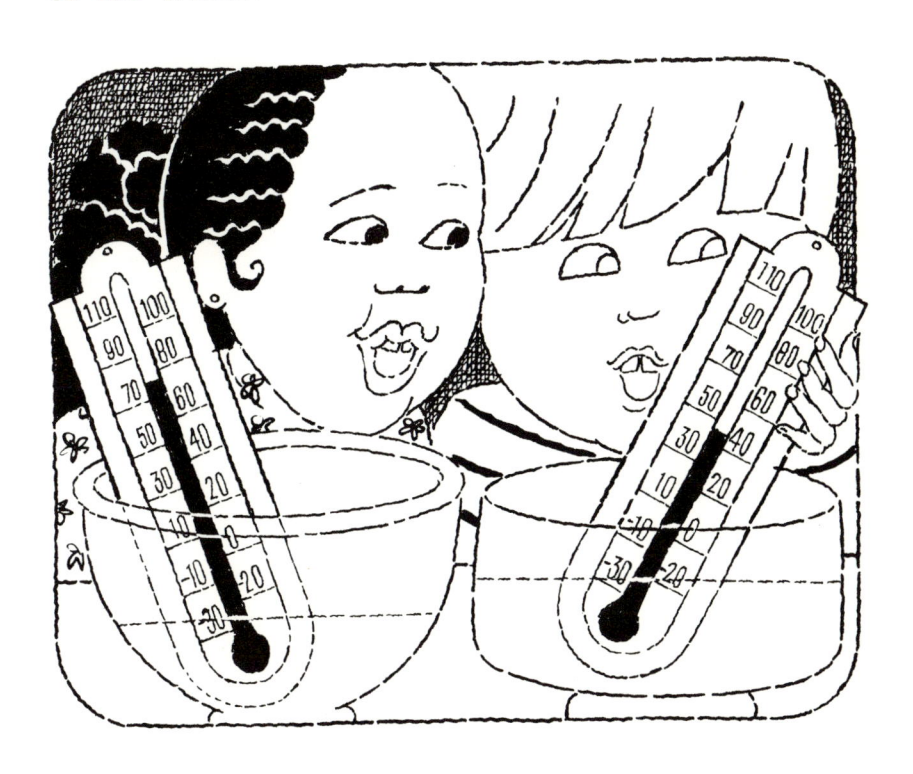

Now do this. Hold your thermometer in the air
in the kitchen for a few minutes. Do you see
the alcohol rising in the tube?

What makes this happen? The *warm air* in the
room does. It warms the alcohol in
the thermometer. This makes the alcohol expand
and rise in the tube.

When the alcohol stops rising, write down the
numeral that is next to the top of the red line.
Now—put the thermometer into the refrigerator.
After five minutes, take it out. Look at it.
You see that the alcohol has gone down in the tube.

What makes it happen? The *cold air* in the
refrigerator does. It makes the alcohol
in the thermometer contract. The alcohol in the
tube moves back toward the bulb.

When it stops moving, write down the numeral
you see next to the top of the red line.
These numerals tell you the temperature
of the air in the room and the temperature
of the air in the refrigerator.

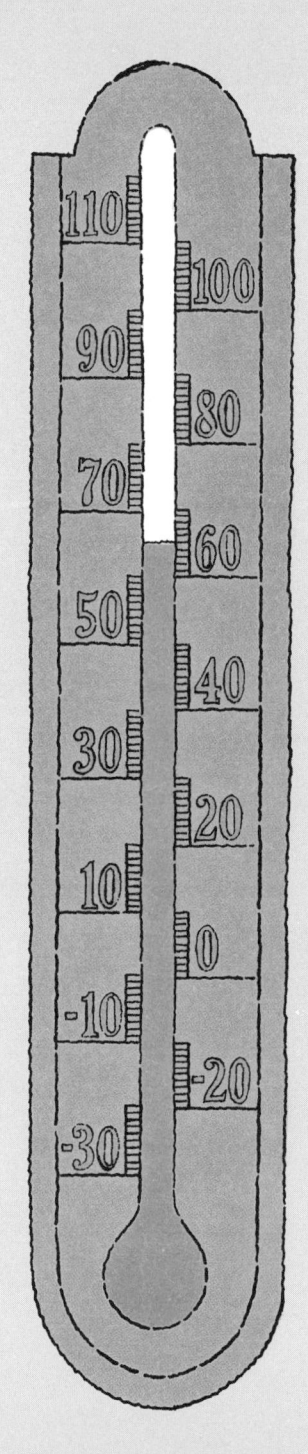

The numerals on the thermometer
are a scale that shows
the *degrees* (0) of temperature.

The scale on your
outdoor thermometer is called the
Fahrenheit (Fair-en-hite) scale.

The higher the temperature,
the higher the number of degrees
you read on the scale.

The lower the temperature,
the lower the number of degrees
you read on the scale.

We call the *degree*
our unit of measure
of temperature.
And—anyone who uses it
can get a careful measurement.

So—we write *65 degrees*
like this: 65°.

You can use your
outdoor thermometer to measure
the temperature of the air
in winter and in summer.

Do you know how cold water that comes
from melting ice is? It is easy to find out.

Put a bowl of ice cubes on the kitchen table.
Place your thermometer into the bowl.
Make sure the ice covers the bulb of the
thermometer. After 20 minutes, when water
covers the bulb, read the numeral that is next
to the top of the red line.

You see that it is at the 32° mark.
This tells you that the temperature
of the water from melting ice cubes is 32°.

We say that the melting point of ice is 32°
on the Fahrenheit scale.

Now—let the container of ice, with the
thermometer in it, stand in the room for
one hour. What happens to the ice?
All of it melts and becomes water.
The warmer air in the room makes the ice melt.

What happens to the temperature of the water?
It rises. The warmer air in the room keeps
warming up the water in the container.

The temperature of the water keeps rising.
It stops when it has the same temperature
as the air in the room.

So you see—you can use your thermometer
to measure the temperature of air and water.

In the wintertime, you may hear the weatherman say, "It is very, very cold outdoors. The temperature is 15°."

What does this mean?

Find the 32° mark on your thermometer. This is the freezing point of water.

Now find the 15° mark.
When the temperature of the air outdoors is 15°, the weather is really 17° colder than the temperature at which water freezes.
This is really a very cold day!

Sometimes a thermometer has a silvery liquid in the tube. This liquid is *mercury*.

Mercury is a liquid metal and—it works in the same way that the alcohol in your thermometer works.

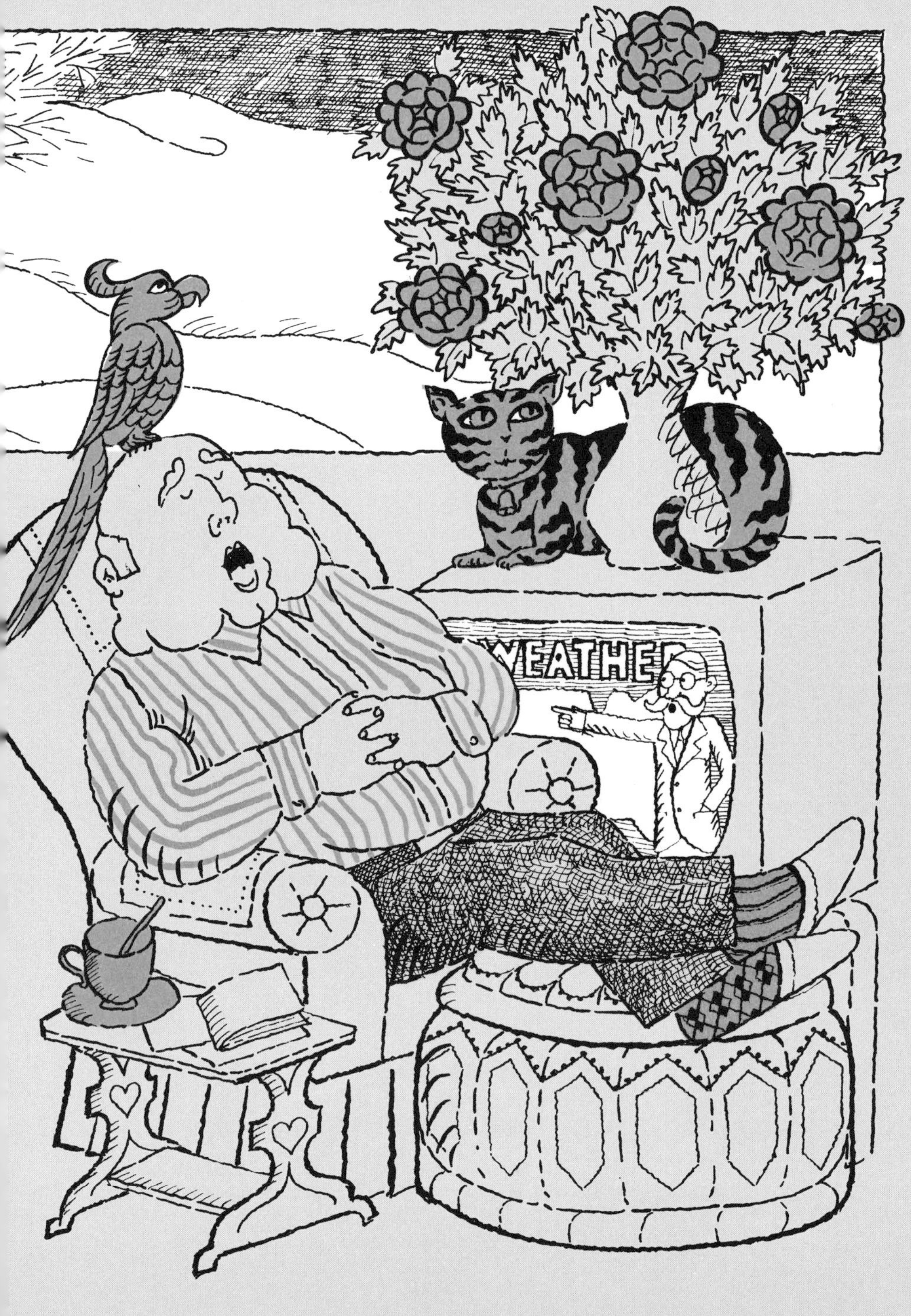

WEATHE

Who uses thermometers to measure temperature carefully?

The weatherman does—when he tells you the temperature of the air outdoors.

Manufacturers do—when they use special metal thermometers to see if they have the correct hot temperatures in their huge ovens to help them make metals, plastics, asphalt, steel and many, many other things.

Bakers do—when they use special metal thermometers to measure the temperature of the hot air in their ovens to help bake their breads, rolls and cakes.

Food market clerks do—when they set their freezers and coolers at cold temperatures to keep foods from spoiling.

Doctors do—when they take people's temperatures.

Mother does—when she roasts meat in the kitchen oven.

And—you do—when you measure the temperature of the water in your fish tank to make sure that it is just right for your tropical fish.

47

Do you think that scientists can send spaceships into orbit around Earth and land our astronauts on the moon if they had to *guess* when they measure—time, distances, weights and temperatures?

Of course they could not!
They can do these wonderful and exciting things because—they have invented and improved measuring instruments that help them get more careful measurements.

So you see—you, too, need to use the measuring instruments that scientists invented when you want to get careful measurements of time, distance, weight and temperature.